Mary Jelkovsky

100 Days of Self-Love

Journaling Prompts to Help You Calm
Self-Criticism and Love Who You Are

BLUE·STAR
PRESS

Copyright © 2022 by Mary Jelkovsky
Published by Blue Star Press
PO Box 5622, Bend, OR 97708
contact@bluestarpress.com | www.bluestarpress.com

Cover Art: Sabina Fenn

ISBN 9781950968794

Printed in Colombia

10 9 8 7 6 5 4 3 2 1

This journal
belongs to:

....

....

....

Introduction

If someone asked you, "Who do you love?" would you ever think to reply, "Myself"?

For too long, I never made my own list. In the rare moments that I even thought about self-love, I believed that it was reserved for people who were perfect and beautiful and all the things I was . . . convinced that I was not. I always told myself, "I'll be happy when (insert some arbitrary standard or expectation here that, even when met, would never truly satisfy me)." Thankfully, after years of consistent therapy, mindset coaching, wisdom books, and an ongoing commitment to being kinder to myself, I've been able to undo some of those deep-rooted, unsupportive beliefs about myself.

In my first book, *The Gift of Self-Love*, I write about how I stopped basing my worth on how others perceived me and healed the subliminal feeling of not-enoughness. I emphasize how, in attempts to have more, do more, and make more, we forget to give ourselves permission to just *be*. For many of us who have been encouraged to work hard, to achieve big goals, and to strive for success, the idea of *just being* may seem scary. It's not that having goals and aspirations is bad, but the biggest mistake people make is believing that approval is synonymous with love. The truth is, there is nothing we must do to "earn" self-love. Just as you love your friends, family, and significant others for who they are, you too deserve to love—or at the very least to accept—yourself for who you are. Love is already there, in your heart and soul and body. The hardest part is channeling it toward yourself.

If you're anything like me, you may have done similar work and had similar realizations about self-love. Like how maybe, just maybe, losing those "last ten pounds" is not the solution to curing body shame. Or how taking care of everyone besides yourself is a surefire way toward resentment, exhaustion, and self-abandonment. And that your mental health and well-being are more important than other people's opinions of you. Perhaps you logically know these things in your mind, but it's still hard to feel them in your heart. There are gaps to fill between learning, knowing, feeling, believing, and practicing self-love.

Love is more than an emotion. It's an energy that is both our life force and source. It's seen and experienced, felt and expressed, received and given. It is an energetic practice that gets solidified through the actions we take. Sometimes self-loving actions involve making a dramatic change in your life, like leaving an unfulfilling job, a not-so-great relationship, or an inhospitable situation of any sort. But most times, self-love entails taking more gentle micro-steps, like becoming aware of your default thought patterns, healthily processing your feelings, and giving yourself more grace, especially during difficult times. It's recognizing when you're too damn hard on yourself and vowing to treat yourself tenderly.

The prompts in the pages to come will help you bridge the gap between self-love as a big, vague, esoteric concept and how it shows up in your daily life. The book is split up into different categories, each integral to our lives and each worth exploring to deepen your self-awareness. When it comes to self-love, though, there is a tremendous amount of overlap between the categories. It's difficult to draw clear lines when we are fluid and multifaceted individuals navigating a complex and colossal world. Still, we try. Here are the categories we'll cover in this journal:

1. **Your purpose**. Because it's often what drives you.
2. **Your identity**. Because how you define yourself creates your character.
3. **Your people**. Because connection is vital, and the people we surround ourselves with influence how we think and feel about ourselves.
4. **Your habits**. Because you become what you repeat.
5. **Your body**. Because you deserve to feel good in the vessel that carries you.
6. **Your mind**. Because building mental strength deserves its own space.
7. **Your heart**. Because some themes require a little more emotional exploration.

Many of the questions will ask you to examine beliefs, challenge social norms, and reflect on the attitudes, experiences, and habits that shaped who you are today. The process of exploring your answers might be messy, but that discomfort is intentional and necessary to deepen your awareness and expand your perspective. You may be wondering how this relates to self-love, and the simple answer is that you can't love yourself if you don't know yourself. By gaining deeper insight into who you are, you'll see that there is so much of you to love.

I've constructed this book to include 100 prompts to help you build a solid, foundational practice of self-love in your life. However, there is no "right" way to use this book. You can do each entry in order or jump around. You can do a page a day or take a few weeks off and come back. Function takes precedence over form, especially as it empowers you to reflect on who you are and reframe how you think, see, and feel about yourself. You might find that some days you'll be called to a particular page; I invite you to jump around to different topics, depending on what you're going (read: growing) through.

I promise that these prompts won't be cheesy quotes or basic questions, but rather brief musings followed by an invitation to self-reflect and explore the topic at hand. Don't try to force anything. Instead, put pen to paper—or just be present in the moment—and find what you discover when you let go and let flow.

As you journey through this book, remember that you are already whole and worthy and wonderful. This journal is a metaphorical multivitamin, a daily dose of self-love meant to help you calm self-criticism and love who you are. I encourage you to write, own, and feel anything you need to because to heal, you must first be real. Don't be afraid to cry on the pages, breathe through the struggles, yell to release tension, dance to celebrate epiphanies big and small, and laugh at the absurdity of being human.

Allowing yourself to be loved unconditionally—by yourself and by others—will be met with less resistance and more ease as you unfold into your most authentic self. This journal is part of that natural unfolding. In a world filled with distractions that drive us away from our center, this is a guide to coming back home to yourself and enjoying the more peaceful stay. And next time you think about all the people you love, you will have the courage to include yourself.

Understand the Self-Love Formula

Have you ever thought about what self-love means practically? What it looks like and feels like?

Before we dive into building a sustainable self-love practice, it's important to understand the main concepts that comprise self-love: self-esteem, self-worth, and self-compassion. Self-esteem—how confident you feel in certain areas of your life—is circumstantial. Self-worth refers to how you feel about yourself, and self-compassion is what you think, say, and do to show yourself love. All three of these combined create a holistic approach to self-love. If we were to put this into a formula, it would look like this:

Self-Love = Self-Esteem + Self-Worth + Self-Compassion

My hope is that this breakdown gives you a clear representation of an abstract concept as you move through this journal. If you wish to go deeper, I explore these concepts further in my first book, *The Gift of Self-Love*. But it's also import-ant to have your own definition of self-love. What does self-love mean to you? What does it look like and, most importantly, *feel* like? Essentially, how do you know when you're living, breathing, and embodying self-love?

heart

Craft "I Am" Statements

Purpose isn't just about what you do for work. You are so much more than your occupation, but society tends to put emphasis on our careers. All of us have more than one role, and we are so much more than we give ourselves credit for. Whenever I'm feeling lost with my purpose in life, I work on expanding what purpose means to me and recognizing that even if I'm feeling lost in my career, I'm living my purpose in other ways.

I do this by writing "I am" statements. These are not affirmations, but rather a list of roles you embody in your life. They could be related to your career, but they extend into your relationships, hobbies, and interests, too. Here is a list of some of my "I am" statements.

I am a big sister. I am a loyal friend. I am a daughter. I am a dog mom. I am a podcaster. I am a creator. I am a public speaker. I am an author. I am an avid reader. I am a soul seeker. I am a world traveler. I am a lifelong student.

Your turn:

I am . . .

purpose

Channel Your Authentic Self

The meaning of the phrase "authentic self" is often taken for granted: what does it mean to live authentically in a world that ruthlessly demands we live according to other people's expectations?

After I hosted my first international self-love retreat, a few of the girls and I extended the trip to visit an island near Bali. At sunset, we were sitting on the front of a boat, sailing the Indian Ocean, when suddenly, ocean water started relentlessly spraying in our faces. We couldn't even talk because the water was coming at us so fast! All we could do was hold on for dear life and laugh our butts off while watching each other get absolutely soaked with saltwater. I felt true joy, and most importantly, I felt my most authentic self: not caring about what I looked like, surrounded by supportive female friends, and surrendering to that chaotic yet delightful experience.

Recall a time when you felt the most like "you," when you felt connected to the present moment and at peace with who you were. Imagine that moment. What were you doing? Who were you with? When and where were you? And most importantly, what were you feeling?

identity

Feel at Home

For my twenty-fourth birthday, I hosted my first gathering in my home. The last time I could remember getting together with more than four friends at a house must have been a childhood slumber party—I was long overdue.

The get-together was inspired by my word of the year: *home*. To me, home is not about the place you live but the people you're with, not just physically but in spirit. In Russian, my mother tongue, the word **"родной"** (pronounced *rod-noy*) doesn't have a direct translation in English, but it is a term of endearment used to describe someone who feels like home. They don't have to be related to you by blood, but they feel like a native part of your soul.

Who feels like home to you, and why?

people

Invest in Basic Self-Care

~~~~~~~~~~~~~~~~

Every self-help book should have a disclaimer: "Do not read this book unless you're already engaging in basic self-care. This includes, but is not limited to, sleeping well, drinking water, laughing often, crying when needed, and eating at least one green vegetable per day."

So often we think that something deeper is wrong with us when we're actually just tired, dehydrated, taking ourselves too seriously, not allowing ourselves to feel our feelings, or even forgetting to munch on some edible plants (the non-hallucinatory kind, I mean). We turn to fad diets, fancy creams, and motivational speeches in search of an external solution to our internal problems, but none of that stuff will ever work better than prioritizing basic self-care. Don't confuse simplicity with ineffectiveness. Basic self-care is not always sexy, but you must love yourself enough to give yourself the essentials before turning to the enhancers.

What basic self-care habits can you add into your day?

Experience Your Body

We spend too much time and energy thinking about how our bodies look to other people. This hyper-focus on our body's external appearance keeps us from feeling comfortable in our skin.

We can spend our entire lives trying to alter our bodies, hoping that the approval and validation will make us feel more accepted and loved. But doing so will only reaffirm that we're basing our worth off of other people's perceptions. Confidence gained from fleeting looks won't last, especially as our bodies change naturally throughout life: during puberty, pregnancy, menopause, illness, aging, and other inevitable changes. "Feeling pretty" is not a feeling at all, but rather a reflection of how we value ourselves based on our perceived beauty. Even the term "body image" is misleading. The body is not an image; it's an experience! The key to healing our relationships with our bodies is realizing that the body is not meant to be looked at—it's meant to be lived in.

What would happen if you stopped worrying about what others see when they look at you? How can you instead focus on what your body allows you to do, see, feel, and experience?

Ask Yourself Questions

~~~~~~~~~

There's a reason lawyers, psychologists, and parents alike frequently ask questions: questions capture our attention, inevitably compelling us to think only about the answer. Posing questions is a powerful tool that can be used for anything from fostering connection to stimulating innovation. And we can use it on ourselves, too, particularly in our self-talk.

When you ask yourself a question, your mind instinctively starts coming up with answers, solutions, and even inventions. For example, instead of telling yourself, "I'm so overwhelmed," you can ask yourself, "What would help me feel more at ease?" Sometimes the questions that sound the most ridiculous or "out there" are the ones that prime our brains for the most creative solutions.

Congratulations! You have unlocked the secret behind this self-love journal. All I'm doing is asking you questions to help you discover your own answers. Hopefully, the more you journal with the help of these prompts, the more you can build the habit of asking yourself questions in your daily self-talk.

What's on your mind right now that you can rephrase into a question? Write down your question and then see how you can answer it.

mind

Recognize That You Are Enough

Feeling that I am "enough" has always been my biggest challenge. Am I good enough for healthy, loving relationships? Am I worthy of having people read my writing and take my advice? Am I working hard enough? Am I achieving enough?

My first instinct is often to "do" something about these thoughts, to somehow "fix" them. You know, throw myself into work, laboriously crossing things off my to-do list in the name of productivity. Post on social media to get reassurance that I'm "liked." Watch a video or listen to a podcast, hoping to find some "motivation." All these approaches have me searching outside myself for reassurance that can only be found within.

When it comes to self-worth, there is nothing to "do." In fact, the more you try to do things to prove your worth, the more disconnected you'll feel from the truth.

The truth is, you are enough, you have always been enough, and you will always be enough exactly the way you are. Embody that truth and fall in love with who you are.

What habits, beliefs, or expectations must you let go of to reaffirm that you are enough?

heart

Find a Purpose Beyond Yourself

People say, "Follow your passion, and the money will come," but not everyone has found their passion, let alone has the privilege to be paid for it. In an era of digital nomads and do-only-what-you-love messaging, I'm here to tell you that it's okay if your job is simply a means to an end.

That's why this section of the journal focuses on purpose and not passion or work. Purpose is what keeps you going when the passion dies or the work becomes tedious. Purpose often gives your life meaning, a goal that extends beyond yourself. Your purpose can be as esoteric as "I want to express my creativity and inspire others through my art" or as revolutionary as "I want to heal generational trauma, so that it ends with me." Your purpose is a living entity; as you evolve, your purpose will evolve with you.

Here are three questions to help you explore your purpose:

1. **What brings me joy?**
2. **What makes me angry?**
3. **What am I willing to struggle for?**

purpose

Find Inspiration to Be Yourself

Your identity boils down to this question: when do you feel the most inspired to be yourself?

My identity as a big sister resonates deeply with me because my little sister inspires me to be silly, goofy, fun, creative, artistic, confident, and free. I also identify with being a writer because stringing together words that explain exactly what I'm thinking, feeling, and exploring inspires me to connect deeply with both myself and others.

You may identify with being a gardener because it inspires you to be grounded in nature. Or with your occupation because it inspires you to work hard, collaborate with others, and bring to life projects you're proud of. Or maybe you identify with a certain community in which you meet like-minded people who encourage acceptance. These are the kinds of identities worth holding onto, while those that don't light you up can be let go and left for someone else.

You don't have just one identity; you have many identities, illuminated by moments when you feel inspired to be yourself. What are some of your identities, and what do they inspire within you?

identity

Connect with Others

~~~~~~~~~~

When I was fourteen, I accompanied my mom to a fancy Christmas party where a bunch of so-called important people had gathered—doctors, lawyers, philanthropists. But one high-spirited man stood out as the life of the party. I watched him all night as he started conversations with the people around him, taking a genuine interest in their lives.

After learning that I spoke Russian, he said to me: "Mary, learn more languages because languages connect you to people." Coming from a man who seemed like the walking embodiment of human connection, his words really stuck with me.

You don't need to start learning a new language tomorrow, but fostering more connection with the people around you is powerful. Today, make a list of people you want to connect with and journal about what you might do to feel closer to them.

people

Build Sustainable Habits

~~~~~~~~~~~~~~

All throughout high school and into college, I was obsessed with getting "healthy." My conception of health was highly influenced by diet culture and beauty standards that focused more on achieving a certain appearance than on promoting ultimate well-being. As I spent years unlearning my disordered behaviors and healing my relationship to food and my body, I had to connect my physical health to my mental well-being. For me, that meant gaining weight, resting more, moving my body in a restorative way, and eating a variety of foods in sufficient quantities. I learned that true healthy living is usually not how it's portrayed in movies, in magazines, or on social media. Health is intricate, interconnected, and deeply individual. It's about building sustainable habits that bring you joy, promote longevity, and care for your body.

What does healthy mean to you? What healthy habits would be sustainable, joyful, and self-loving to you? How can you incorporate them into your daily routine?

Eat Intuitively

"You can't live a full life on an empty stomach." This saying served as a constant reminder to me as I was relearning how to nourish my body properly after nearly a decade of disordered eating. For so long, I resisted my body's hunger and ignored its fullness, thinking that food was something to be controlled, counted, and restricted. I'd been programmed to believe that my natural need to eat couldn't be trusted: everything I watched, read, and learned—from movies to magazines to my own mother's advice—reinforced my disordered eating.

It wasn't until I found intuitive eating, an approach to eating that encourages people to accept their bodies and eat without guilt or shame, that I finally learned to make peace with food. Intuitive eating begins by listening to your body and trusting that it knows what it needs.

Think about your relationship with food. How can you listen to your body more and prioritize nourishing it in an intuitive, self-loving way?

Like Yourself

~~~~~~~~~~~~~~~~~~~

In my first long-term relationship, my then boyfriend told me, "I love you, but I don't like you." These words cracked me open and altered how I view love in relationships: sometimes it's not enough to *love* someone; you must also *like* them. The same can apply to your relationship with yourself. True love is unconditional but liking yourself (or the person you're with) is important, too. The person you spend the most time with is yourself, so if you're struggling to like yourself, you must dig deeper to find things you like about yourself, or make yourself into a person you like.

During hard moments, try repeating this:

I like who I am and the person I'm becoming.

What do you like about yourself? Do you have one of those laughs that make everyone else laugh? Are you kind, open-minded, trustworthy, or ambitious? What personality traits, quirks, or gifts do you embrace about yourself?

Revel in Small Moments of Joy

When I stare out into the ocean and realize that all I see is not all there is. When I watch my little sister feel proud of her art. When I think there is no more chocolate left, only to find one more piece that's even more enjoyable in its unexpectedness. When my dog buries his head into my body as I pet him. When I smell someone I love. When I complete something that I've put my whole heart into. When I notice that my hibiscus plant has blossomed. When the temperature of my tea is just right. When I spend my nights reading and my mornings writing. When I laugh about something silly and other people start laughing because of how hard I'm laughing. When it starts raining, and I don't care if I get wet. When my fruit bowl is full. When I see an elderly couple holding hands.

These are small moments of joy that make my heart happy. What are your small moments of joy?

Choose Values Over Labels

When juggling different roles and wearing many hats in life, it's easy to get boxed into conventional labels like girlfriend, spouse, parent, child, employee, etc. Notice how these descriptors only address who you are in relation to others. They fail to evoke who you are at your core, outside of other people.

Core values, on the other hand, are heart-centered guiding principles that serve as the foundation of your identity. They summarize what's important to you and what drives you toward your purpose.

My core values are family, freedom, fun, leadership, and love. I try to ensure that my actions, my relationships, and how I conduct myself in the world align with my core values. Only then can I feel the most fulfilled, purposeful, and authentic. If something interferes with my core values, I reevaluate the situation and recalibrate my efforts to my values. If I'm conflicted about a decision, I revisit my values and ask myself which most aligns with what I stand for.

Determine five of your core values—what you hold as most important to you. You can search for a list of options online if you'd like help. Once you select them, memorize them and repeat them to yourself often. Let your values guide your decisions.

Gain Confidence through Clarity

Sometimes, the ways we describe ourselves are simple, set in stone, and accepted by society. Other times, they're more complex, seemingly contradictory, and rejected by those who don't understand. For example, I'm proud of my identity as a first-generation American with immigrant parents, but I sometimes feel insecure when asked about my Russian culture and Jewish ethnicity.

Perhaps you're proud of and confident in certain aspects of your identity, and there are other parts that you're still exploring. Sometimes all you need to gain a little clarity is to write it all out. Clarity is a prerequisite for confidence. If you're unclear about your identity, you'll have trouble finding confidence in it. But even being able to say, "I don't know—I haven't figured that out about myself yet" is a sign of clarity! Once you're comfortable with not knowing, you can either try to fill in the gaps or make peace with existing in the unknown.

As you think about your identity, consider how you'd describe yourself to some-one who doesn't know you. Which are the parts of your identity that you're clear on, and which are the parts of your identity that you're unsure about?

identity

Consider Your True Support System

I've often encountered this popular saying: "You can't love someone else until you love yourself first." Although there is a small element of truth to it, I don't entirely agree with this notion. Does a mother not fully love her children unless she's madly in love with herself? What about people who struggle with mental health conditions? Is their love for others somehow not valid due to chemical imbalances that make it extra difficult to love themselves?

There are certainly people in my own life—my mom, my sister, my best friend—whom I love dearly and unconditionally, even when I'm feeling less than myself. Their love reinforces that I am worthy of loving myself.

No one can fix or heal the way you feel about yourself, but there will be people who believe in you, nudge you in the right direction, and teach you how to receive love.

Today, think about your support system. Who in your life has been there for you, and what have they taught you about love?

Move Your Body

~~~~~~~~~~~~~~~~~

When we view exercise as something we "have" to do, then we'll probably choose activities we don't like and struggle to stay consistent. This leads to a cycle of beating ourselves up, giving up for a while, and bouncing from one extreme to the other. However, when we reframe movement as something we "get" to do, then it becomes more enjoyable, easier to stick with, and more sustainable as a long-term habit.

To me, the words "work out" or "exercise," when used in the context of physical fitness, connote that moving our bodies is an obligatory chore rather than a pleasurable privilege. Movement is different from exercise because it doesn't limit us to stereotypical gym workouts; movement can be anything from having a solo dance party in our rooms to playing Frisbee with our families. Why force yourself into draining, discouraging, and sometimes even painful exertions when you can focus on movement that's joyful, energizing, and restorative?

How can you move your body in a way that feels good today?

habits

Be Open to Sexual Intimacy

Self-love is the elixir of sexual intimacy, empowering you to choose and open up to the right partner. You must have enough love for yourself so that intimacy with another reaffirms the love inside of you, rather than steals and depletes it. When we are unkind to our bodies, we suppress our sexuality, and the mind-body-heart connection becomes difficult to recalibrate. Here are some ways to work on sexual intimacy:

1. Focus on accepting your naked body by looking at it with adoration, as if you were a Renaissance painting and the strokes of your figure a masterpiece.

2. Engage in self-pleasure. As you explore, pay attention to what you like and what you don't like, what makes you expand and what makes you contract.

3. Inhabit a safe place during sexual intimacy, both in your environment and in the person you're with.

4. Practice being authentic in the bedroom, communicating your needs, wants, and desires without shame or blame.

How do you feel about your sexual intimacy?

body

Don't Fall for "Perfect"

~~~~~~~~~~

As a recovering perfectionist, I remind myself daily that the word "perfect" is not meant to describe people. *Merriam-Webster* defines perfection as "having no mistakes or flaws," which contradicts what it means to be human.

When you spend your life chasing something nonexistent, like perfection, you'll constantly feel inadequate and exhausted. The more you try to become this unachievable "perfect person," the more your efforts (read: obsession) will take you away from the present moment.

Your presence is far more necessary than your perfection. Your kids won't remember how your hair looked or if the carpet was cleaned; they'll remember if you were there to play with them. Your boss won't care if you drive yourself crazy crafting the perfect presentation; they just need you to show up confidently and courageously. Your partner does not need the most extravagant anniversary gift; all they want is your heart.

Where can you let go of perfection and replace it with your authentic presence?

Have Compassion During Low Days

Many of us have expectations of what self-love looks like. Maybe that's waking up in the morning, loving what we see in the mirror, and feeling confident in ourselves as we move through our day. But does that mean we've failed on the days we don't feel that way? Or that we're not cut out for self-love and that we should just give up?

No. You can't fail if you're trying. Your "best" will vary in relation to your physical, emotional, and spiritual capacity at any moment. Have compassion and patience for yourself because no matter how hard you work at self-love, there will still be low days filled with uncertainty and doubt. Each day will be different, but what will not change is how worthy, wonderful, and whole you are regardless.

As with anything in life, the goal is not to have everything figured out—it's to make peace with uncertainty. The space between what you know and what you don't know is where the learning and growing happens. Take a moment to hold that truth in your heart.

What did your best look like yesterday? What does it look like today?

Never Stop Growing

My high school French teacher, Madame, loved to bake. Madame would bribe us to get good grades by promising homemade cake pops to whomever aced their exams. Many of us stayed after class to eat our treats and chat with our beloved teacher.

Madame, who was fifty at the time and had been teaching half her life, would often tell us, "I want to be a baker when I grow up." She had cracked a code in life that has left me inspired since: we're never done growing or dreaming. No one is obligated to pursue one path for the rest of their life, no matter how old they are or how stuck they feel. As kids, we dream about the entire future ahead of us. Then, after we graduate and get jobs and unexplained back pain, it sinks in that we're already "grown up," and we stop allowing ourselves to dream. But those who dare to dream are inspired in the present while simultaneously planting seeds for the future.

Who or what do you want to be when you grow up? Don't limit yourself to career choices here; write down anything and everything you aspire to be.

purpose

Get to Know Yourself

When I was a teenager, fitness was my entire identity. My community was centered around gym culture, and when I became a bikini fitness competitor, I composed my online presence with workout videos, "progress" pics, and endless self-scrutiny.

After years of restrictive dieting and obsessive exercising, my extreme lifestyle caught up to me. My body, mind, and spirit were exhausted. I ended up leaving the bodybuilding industry, which was healthy and necessary. But quitting came with side effects: I gained weight and felt like I lost my entire identity. If I wasn't "the fitness girl" with the "perfect" body, who the hell was I? If I didn't get approval for my body, how would I ever be accepted and loved?

A big part of my healing involved discovering who I truly was so that I could leave behind what society told me I "should" be, in favor of my own passions. This is an ongoing process for me. By allowing for playful fluidity, gentle curiosity, and endless exploration, we can tap into our true selves.

Knowing that your own identity will always be evolving, how can you embody playful fluidity, gentle curiosity, and endless exploration?

Don't You Dare

~~~~~~~~~~~~~~~~

I wrote this poem in my journal one day, and I want to pass it on to you:

Don't you dare,
for one more second,
surround yourself with people
who are not aware
of the beauty
that you hold.

Who in your life embraces your beauty? Who brings out the best in you?

Prioritize Self-Care

Self-love begins as a mindset, an energy, and an overall appreciation for yourself, but it is actualized, solidified, and practiced through self-care. You wouldn't expect someone else to believe you when you say, "I love you" if you did nothing to show them love, so you mustn't expect that from yourself.

It's easy to compromise on self-care when you've been putting everyone else's needs above your own your whole life, but you must be your own priority. You must follow through on what you say you're going to do for yourself. You must create habits that support your mental health, including partaking in hobbies for fun and enjoyment. When you're struggling, turn to your journal and give yourself pep talks. Be honest with yourself, knowing when you need to give yourself a loving kick in the butt. Self-care is not a luxury—it's a necessity.

How can you prioritize self-care today and make a habit of it moving forward?

habits

Explore Pleasure

~~~~~~~~~~~~~~~~~~~~

Pleasure . . . ahhh, I love that word. When you say it out loud, it sounds so *juicy*.

That first sip of coffee on a brisk winter day. The smell of your favorite fall-scented candle. The warmth of hugging your pet after coming home from a long day. The sound of your partner's heart beating as you lie on their chest. That feeling of relinquishing control and surrendering to your body's wishes.

Experiencing pleasure helps us tear down the layers of shame we've absorbed from society, reconnect to our body's innate wisdom, and lose ourselves in deep, raw, authentic self-expression.

When you hear the word "pleasure," what thoughts, feelings, or emotions come up for you? Does "pleasure" sound like something sweet and luscious or like something icky and wrong? Does it make you uncomfortable? Or does it make you squeal with delight? Do you instantly think of sexual pleasure? Or do you think of the little moments that make you feel warm and tingly inside? Do you feel you're worthy of pleasure?

Be a Neutral Nancy, Not a Positive Polly

Although positive thinking can be an effective approach to confidence building, being a Positive Polly can sometimes backfire. Studies show that people who struggle with anxiety and depression (or those who are prone to self-defeating spirals) actually feel worse when they try to force themselves to say positive affirmations. Imagine that in despair, you share your pain with a friend, only for them to say, "Everything will be fine! Just think positively!" It's unhelpful, invalidating, and isolating. Psychologists call this phenomenon "toxic positivity." It's important to allow ourselves to feel the full range of human emotions without using positivity to suppress the "bad" ones.

Shifting into "neutral thinking," by inviting in thoughts that are more representative of reality, can be helpful. If you're struggling to accept your body, looking at yourself in the mirror and chanting, "I love my body" probably won't help because it won't feel genuine. Instead, step away from the mirror and tell yourself that you don't have to like how your body looks to appreciate what it does for you.

How can you employ this more neutral and realistic self-talk as you practice reframing your mindset?

Be Proud of Yourself

Every time someone says, "I'm proud of you," tears start welling up in my eyes. Those words hit straight at my heart. Maybe I didn't hear it enough as a kid. Maybe I don't tell myself that enough as an adult. Maybe you don't either.

I don't know what you've been through or what brought you here, but if you're reading this right now, if you're on this journey, I'm proud of you. I'm proud of you for surviving every difficult situation you've encountered and for allowing the experiences to shape you into the remarkable human you are today. I'm proud of you for having the courage to keep going and for having the discernment to know when it's time to quit, to leave, to choose yourself. I'm proud of you for enduring the wounds that have already faded into scars and the wounds that are healing as we speak.

As my favorite author, Paulo Coelho, said, "Be proud of your scars. They remind you that you have the will to live."

What are you proud of yourself for?

heart

Let Go and Let Flow

In a "flow" state, you're fully present in the moment, focused on a single task, and ideas seem to come to you without force. But it takes time to get there. At first, while trying to focus, you may feel like you're dillydallying, but there's a turning point where things feel easier and more pleasant. Flow can occur during any activity—writing, surfing, painting, gardening—but the key is to avoid multitasking, when your attention becomes dispersed and diluted. Only when you're focused on *one* thing can you really let go and let flow.

Sometimes I struggle getting into a flow while writing because I'm tempted by distractions on my phone or my to-do lists. But once I get over that initial hump of resistance, the flow takes over and writing becomes effortlessly enjoyable.

What activities allow you to let go and let flow? How do you feel when you're fully immersed in them?

Unearth the Buried Parts of Yourself

Your identity wasn't created in a vacuum. It greatly depends on your environment, especially how you were raised and the people who surrounded you. Some of us had parents and peers who encouraged our self-expression, allowing us to feel safe exploring ourselves, while others might have felt we needed to suppress our true selves out of fear of rejection. But most of our experiences fall somewhere in the middle: we've been told to be ourselves, but the subtext was "Be yourself to the extent that we can understand and approve of you."

As adults, part of our self-love journey is to unearth the parts of ourselves we buried, form beliefs that are aligned with our values, and cultivate an environment that's safe for us to be authentic. Not only is this healing to our individual inner child, but it's necessary for our growth as adults.

What kind of environment were you raised within? Were you able to be your authentic self?

What kind of environment do you now seek and why?

Learn from Your Mother

I was raised by a single mom who doubled as my best friend. She wasn't perfect, but she's always been the best parent for me. As an adult, aided by therapy, I've engaged in "reparenting my inner child," a practice that fills in the gaps my parents couldn't provide for me. One of those gaps stemmed from my mother's relationship with her body and how that influenced my own.

Watching the most beautiful woman in the world, the one who birthed me, constantly scrutinizing herself in the mirror took a toll on my own body image. I've come to understand that obsessing over weight loss and beauty was my subconscious attempt at connecting with my mother through our shared struggles. She taught me a lot about self-love in other forms, but I had to teach myself about positive body image and heal from my eating disorder on my own.

Our mothers have a lot to teach us about self-love, even if it's by highlighting how *not* to be.

What did your maternal figure teach you about self-love? What do you wish she could have instilled in you?

Practice Joy

To prepare and protect you, your brain uses memories of past experiences to predict future ones. For example, if you got bullied riding the bus as a kid, the sight of a bus might ignite fear. Now, when you see a bus, rather than feeling an emotion at first, a *physical* reaction occurs—heart pounding, palms sweating, adrenaline rushing through you. Then, your brain reacts to these physical sensations, quickly conjuring up an emotion to match—fear. Even if the bully is no longer there, your body remembers your past traumatic experiences, and your brain interprets the adrenaline rush as fear to make you avoid the danger.

But what if, later, you met the love of your life while riding the bus? Your brain is more likely to register that same adrenaline rush as excitement when you have a positive experience attached to it. Your body and brain are so deeply connected. The good news is you can train your brain to be more prone to positive emotions by physically practicing them. For example, you can invite inner peace by taking five minutes to meditate or tap into joy by watching your favorite comedy, which will hopefully make you laugh.

Which positive emotion do you want to feel today, and how will you practice it?

Rest Before You're Tired

As a society, we have a paradoxical relationship with rest: everyone is constantly complaining about how tired they are, yet no one gets enough rest. Have we been raised to prioritize labor over leisure so much that we don't feel like we deserve rest until we've worked hard enough to earn it? Tricia Hersey, founder of the Nap Ministry, created a community around the idea that "Rest is Resistance." Tricia writes that we have been brainwashed by grind culture, capitalism, and white supremacy to believe that we're not enough unless we're always doing something. In a world that tells us to keep going, keep grinding, keep producing, rest *is* resistance. Sleep is self-care. Doing nothing is necessary. We must relax and recharge, not so that we can work more, but to remind ourselves that we have full permission to simply exist, to just be. After all, we are not human doings; we are human *beings*.

Don't wait until you're utterly exhausted; rest *before* you're tired as an act of self-preservation.

What is your relationship with rest like? Do you feel worthy of rest even if you haven't been active or productive?

Give Up the Illusion of Control

When I was little, I was obsessed with rearranging my room. The urge hit me late at night when I was alone with my thoughts. I'd spend hours moving around my furniture and repositioning my tchotchkes, trying to find ways to create order within the chaos of my childhood.

We do this in our minds, too. How many times have you replayed events in your head, thinking about what you should have said or done? Or pieced together the same information repeatedly, trying to make sense of something difficult to process? Like Little Me compulsively rearranging her room, we ruminate on thoughts in our minds, usually fueled by worry, stress, fear, and anxiety.

Just as there's a difference between redecorating your home and moving around the same three pieces of furniture repeatedly, there's a difference between processing and ruminating. Rumination, or repetitive thoughts, gives us the illusion of control, but it's not real. At a certain point, we must let go and let things be as they are.

What have you been ruminating on lately? How can you let go and let things be?

mind

Talk to Your Inner Child

Recently I found a giant box filled with my old journals, yearbooks, and pictures from my childhood and spent hours sifting through it. That night, my partner came home to see me sobbing with a glass of wine in hand and a fluffy pink diary in my lap. I'd stumbled upon parts of myself, events, and experiences that I'd buried so deep, I didn't even have clear remembrance of them until I read the words written by Little Me, when the memories came flooding back. Reading my diaries reminded me of how much I've tried to forget.

Even if there are parts of your past that you buried in your mind to protect your inner child, they still live in your body and in your heart. You don't have to bring out your old journals or try to recall specifics, but trust that your inner child has insights that you've lost sight of (often as a protective coping mechanism). If Little You could talk to you, what would they want you to know? Write a letter from Little You to Big You.

Dear Big Me,

heart

Love,
Little Me

Value Yourself

Whatever you do for work, whether you're a stay-at-home parent, contributing to a company, or growing your own business, how you're compensated for your work must feel like an equal exchange of energy. If you're putting in more than you're compensated for—financially or emotionally—you will eventually become bitter, resentful, and exhausted. By valuing yourself, you stop allowing people or companies to undervalue and underpay you. If you're not being compensated fairly, you have three options: request more compensation, leave the job for a different one, or find or create other benefits that would make your current job worth your while.

Even though it may feel scary to ask for what you're worth, it's essential for setting expectations for what you will (and will not) accept in exchange for your time, energy, and skills.

Are you compensated equitably for what you do? If not, how can you ask for more or find or create benefits—like learning a new skill or building connections—that would make it worth it for you?

purpose

Play Hide-and-Seek

"I don't know who I am anymore . . . I feel like I've lost myself." I've said this to myself, to my best friend, and to my therapist quite a few times, often after being unhappy with a particular circumstance for an extended period. It has been a job that exhausted me to the point where I lost any energy for my hobbies or passions. I've built up resentment from a relationship that sucked me dry. Other times, I found myself doing too much for too many people, trying to please everyone at the expense of myself, and at a certain point, I broke. Or rather, my identity broke under the weight of all the stress and inauthenticity. Eventually, I had to rebuild my foundation and find myself again.

Like self-love, finding yourself is a continuous practice. Even when you feel solid in parts of your identity, there's always more to explore, discover, and unleash within yourself. It's an ongoing game of hide-and-seek where you are both the hider and the seeker.

What parts of yourself have you been hiding? What parts have gotten lost in the shuffle of life? What parts of yourself do you wish to find?

Learn from Your Father

Growing up with an estranged father left me constantly seeking external validation. I thought that if he wouldn't be there for me, then why would anyone else? So, I tried to fill that void with other men in my life—my stepdads, uncles, and even the men I dated—desperate to prove myself lovable.

Some of our deepest parental wounds stem from the chronic absence of a parent, including physical loss, abandonment, and emotional neglect. Dads who are physically present but emotionally absent also have a profound impact on how we view, treat, and accept ourselves. These situations can produce a complex array of emotions—anger, resentment, fear, shame, love—that are difficult to process, work through, and heal from. Approaching this process with compassion can ease the pain and make you even stronger.

How has your father figure influenced your self-love? What do you wish he could have given you?

people

Focus on Today

My aunt knew she wanted to be a dentist since getting her front teeth knocked out on the monkey bars when she was six. She went to college, then dental school, then opened her own practice, fulfilling a purpose she'd had since childhood—helping others get through the pain she'd experienced. I've always been jealous of people who know exactly what they want and have a clear, easy-to-put-into-one-sentence-and-get-nods-of-approval-from-others kind of path for how to get there.

But most people don't grow up knowing what they want to do, and even once they find their path, they face twists, turns, and bouts of uncertainty. There is no one "right" way to pursue your purpose. Here's a good question to help focus on your purpose every day: "What can I do today that will add meaning to my life?" This can be as simple as taking a nap or as grandiose as writing the screenplay for your next movie. Incorporating small, meaningful moments into your daily life can lead you toward the bigger picture of your purpose.

What can you do today that will add meaning to your life?

She Hears You

~~~~~~~~

Your body hears you.

She hears it when you think
"I hate you
I wish I could change you."

She hears it when you think
about skipping breakfast
or missing lunch.

She hears it when you blame Her
without cause
or without reason
because there's never a cause
or a reason
for abusing your home
for mistreating your temple
for neglecting your vessel.

She hears all of it
She absorbs all of it

and She hurts from all of it.

But She also hears it when you say
"I'm sorry, please forgive me.
I'm still learning to love you."

She hears it when you
try to love her
despite the noise
the thoughts
the shame.

She hears it when you
touch Her lovingly
treat Her kindly
trust Her fully.

She hears your efforts.
And to Her,
they mean the world.

What does your body need to hear from you today?

_____
_____
_____
_____
_____
_____
_____
_____
_____

Explore Secondary Emotions

We are taught to chase happiness, believing it's better to feel only "good" and never "bad." But happiness is fleeting, as is anger, sadness, and fear. These primary emotions are reactions, outside of our control and dependent on external circumstances. Chasing happiness and trying to avoid harder emotions is a pointless pursuit. Part of the beauty of being human is experiencing a wide range of nuanced emotion.

Allow for the primary emotions to come as they will, observing them with curiosity and compassion rather than judgment. Then, see if you can identify any secondary emotions, feelings that float up after you've sat with the primary emotions. For example, "I am *angry* at my father" might turn into "I am *hurt* by my father." Secondary emotions will often present as confusing and complex, but once you identify them, you can begin to make peace with them.

The more you acknowledge and accept this full range of human emotion, the more inner peace you'll find.

What primary emotions have come up for you lately? What nuanced secondary emotions have come from the primary ones? Feel free to look up "feelings wheel" online to get more ideas.

mind

Celebrate Breakups

After a horrible breakup, I flew to Bali on a whim, in search of adventure and time to heal. On my first day, I met a couple at the pool who were on their honeymoon. When I told them that I was on my breakup trip, they smiled at me, looked at each other, and in unison exclaimed, "Congratulations!"

Four years later, I got to chatting with a woman in line behind me at a home decor store. She told me that she'd just moved into a new apartment by herself because she was going through a divorce. "Congratulations!" I blurted out, with little hesitation, though instantly I hoped it didn't come off as insensitive. For a second, the woman seemed a bit confused until her face expanded into a proud smile. "Yes," she said, "congratulations to me!"

If you're going through a breakup or have ever experienced heartbreak of any sort, congratulations. You are now stronger, wiser, and free to explore new realms of (self) love.

What have you learned from your most recent heartbreak? How can you allow this breakup to break you open rather than break you down?

Address Impostor Syndrome

Impostor syndrome is the phenomenon of believing you aren't as capable as others perceive you to be. Notably, it disproportionately affects women, especially minorities: these groups are affected by stereotypes, discrimination, and persistent questioning of their abilities, especially in the workplace. Basically, all the times you've been told you don't belong get internalized until you falsely believe that you're not worthy of success.

Early studies on and approaches to impostor syndrome have failed to acknowledge these root causes and instead blame low self-esteem. Impostor syndrome could come from a lack of confidence, but it could also stem from systemic inequalities, an unsupportive work environment, or lack of representation. Once you pinpoint where your impostor syndrome is coming from, you can address it by building up your self-worth, advocating for a more inclusive workplace, and reminding yourself that your achievements help pave the way for others.

Where does your impostor syndrome come from? What can you tell yourself to reaffirm that you are worthy of the success you've already achieved and more prosperity than you can yet imagine?

purpose

Cut the Balloon Strings

~~~~~~~~~~~

When my therapist and I were just getting to know each other, we dug into some of my complex family dynamics in our earliest sessions. To help me understand how attached I was to approval from my family members, she gave me this analogy, which I've paraphrased here:

Picture yourself connected to a bunch of balloons. Each balloon represents an emotional tie to someone or something. They're all pulling you in different directions with their opinions, expectations, and agendas, preventing you from flying your own path. The goal is to slowly snip the strings from each of the balloons, keeping only the balloons that truly represent you. When you let go of the balloons, you will be able to fly on your own.

What balloons do you want to snip away to let your identity soar?

identity

Ask for What You Need

Navigating a relationship without communication is like baking a cake without following a recipe. You're familiar with the ingredients, but how much of each do you add? And in what order? Although you know what a cake should taste like, you didn't have instructions to bake this one properly. You pull it from the oven to find it didn't rise, and it tastes off.

A lack of authentic communication can have the same effect on a relationship: if you don't give others information on how best to attend to your needs, you set unrealistic expectations for the relationship. Learning how to communicate your needs to others will not only strengthen your relationships, but also empower you to become more self-aware and attend to your own unmet needs.

So, what is it that you need from your closest relationships? How can you communicate your needs or support them yourself?

people

Simplify Decisions

As a perpetual overthinker, making decisions is exhausting for me. Having too many choices can backfire, causing stress in many facets of life, both big and small: selecting which schools to attend and classes to enroll in, who to date amid endless swiping, what movies and TV shows to watch, what food to order, and even what path to pursue in life. This indecisiveness contributes to a lack of self-trust and an overall dissatisfaction with our choices.

When my indecisiveness interferes with my well-being, I set an intention to get out of my head and listen to my body for the answers. I ask myself, "Which decision would feel like a sigh of relief?" I look for that feeling of a weight being lifted off my chest and my body exhaling the tension. When making decisions, breathe, listen to your body, and trust yourself.

What decisions are you feeling conflicted or unsure about? Which would feel like a sigh of relief?

Tip: "Try on" the different options and pay attention to which one most relaxes your body when you think about acting on it.

habits

Unsubscribe from Unhealthy Beliefs

After guiding thousands of women on their journeys to body acceptance, I've noticed that most resistance comes from confusing our own feelings about our bodies with society's expectations. The desire to lose weight usually comes from deep-rooted body shame and a belief that losing weight will make us more worthy of love. Because the fatphobic notion that "thinner = better" is perpetuated and reinforced by most aspects of society, it's difficult to distinguish the difference between making healthy choices for ourselves and guilting ourselves into certain behaviors that we've been programmed to think will make us feel beautiful, accepted, and worthy.

If you feel this way, it's not your fault. You've been fed this message your whole life. But what if you didn't have to change your body, or anything about your appearance, to feel whole? Question where your insecurities stem from and consider how you can unsubscribe from certain beliefs that aren't serving you.

Who taught you that your body isn't good enough as it is? If pictures, mirrors, and other people's opinions didn't exist, how would you feel about your body? How can you unsubscribe from negative body-image beliefs?

body

Be Conscious of Word Choice

The concept of positive self-talk is a little misleading because it's not realistic to think, feel, and say only "good" things. We must allow ourselves to process and feel the "bad" thoughts and feelings, too. It's only after we allow and acknowledge the state of things that we can begin to reframe them. Reframing your thoughts doesn't mean that you'll go from "I'm a piece of shit" to "I'm a glorious queen" in one second. That's not positive self-talk. That's forceful self-deception.

Instead, choose thoughts that reflect the experience you're having while allowing yourself room to grow into the experience you want to have. Use words like "practicing," "learning," and "becoming." The words "I am practicing loving myself" may feel more real to you than "I love myself." These types of present-focused phrases close the gap between where you are now and what you're working toward. Self-love is a process, a constant unraveling of your perceived self into your true self.

You can embrace this concept by filling out your own version of the following:

I am practicing . . .
I am learning . . .
I am becoming . . .

Go There

At my retreats, we start by discussing what I call our "Collective Agreements": twelve rules that summarize the expectations and boundaries for our time together. The third Agreement is "I challenge myself to share more than I might normally." Retreats create a safe space for people to let their guards down, break their hearts open, and learn to receive love (including self-love). Sometimes during deep emotional work—in therapy, recovery, relationship building, or even journaling—we subconsciously hold back from "going there" because we are afraid.

We are afraid to feel something that might make us lose control or force us to confront our own facade. We're afraid of being seen because we're afraid of being rejected. So, we end up holding back from both ourselves and each other.

But if we're so afraid of feeling something big, we will never be able to fully heal. And if we're too afraid of being rejected, we will never have the opportunity to feel accepted. The only way is to lean into that fear and "go there."

What are you unwilling to feel? What are you afraid of? How can you go there?

heart

Stop Guilting Yourself

If you're anything like me, you put pressure on yourself to do things you feel you *should* do but that can't really bring yourself to do. These things hang over our heads—from finishing the dozens of books on our nightstands to replying to messages we've put off, from calling our parents to wearing clothes that are only collecting dust in our closets—serving as constant reminders of what we've failed to do.

To live our lives with purpose, with more intention and self-love, we must stop guilting ourselves into doing things we don't truly care about. Donate the books you don't want to read; remind yourself that your inbox can wait and you don't owe anyone 24/7 access to you; and get rid of those clothes that don't make you feel like your best self.

What are some tasks, pressures, or expectations you can release from your physical or mental space? Once you write them down, either physically remove them from your life or cross them off this paper to metaphorically clear your precious mental real estate.

purpose

Be All of You

~~~~~~~~~~

When someone says, "You're too much," they're really saying, "I don't feel enough." If your self-expression bothers someone else, then they are free to look away or leave your space. Their feelings about you are not your responsibility. The more you try to twist your identity into something that others accept, the more you risk losing your authentic self.

Someone who is threatened by your self-expression—someone who thinks you're too much or not enough or too this or too that—doesn't understand you because they have not yet learned to understand themselves. Let yourself be their mirror. Let them see what they have yet to heal. Let them be threatened by your light until they learn to shine on their own.

In the meantime, keep being all of you, knowing that you are never too much for the right people.

Have you ever felt that you're too much? Who or what made you feel that way?

identity

Commit to Your Boundaries

Setting boundaries involves recognizing your limits, communicating them clearly, then holding not only others but yourself accountable. When you set boundaries, do you ever feel guilty or afraid that you'll upset someone if you don't adhere to their wishes? Mental or emotional boundaries are often the hardest because they force you to dig into your own underlying beliefs and to fight the thoughts that wrongfully say you don't deserve rest, respect, personal space, and safety.

Committing to your boundaries requires you to be self-aware and to take responsibility, instead of blaming others, if you haven't clearly communicated those boundaries. This process will force you to trade short-term niceness for long-term kindness. Albeit difficult to implement, setting healthy boundaries will ensure that you prioritize your own needs in a world where you've been taught to bend over backward for others at the expense of yourself.

What boundaries do you struggle with? To whom do you need to communicate your boundaries in a better way?

Use Style for Self-Expression

My whole life I've been quite insecure about my personal style, partially because it's difficult for me to imagine an outfit before seeing it on my body. I've also told myself that I'm a "lost cause" when it comes to fashion, which leads to a discouraging self-fulfilling prophecy. However, when I take the time to put an outfit together that feels representative of myself and my current mood, I feel on top of the world!

Though it's unnecessary and unsustainable to always keep up with the latest trends and "dress to impress," every day presents an opportunity to express yourself through what you wear. When you show up in an outfit that feels representative of you on that day, whether casual or dressed up, you are living in alignment with your authentic self and empowering yourself to be seen for who you are. Style is a form of self-expression and, by extension, self-love.

How would you describe your personal style? Does what you're wearing right now feel aligned with your mood today? What does a quintessential everyday outfit feel like for you, and how can you dress more like yourself on a regular basis?

habits

Identify the Root of Body Shame

A lot of people mistakenly believe that body shame stems from feeling not attractive enough, whether in relation to body size, shape, weight, or overall appearance. But the problem isn't that you don't like how you look; the problem is that our society positions beauty as paramount, especially for women. From our earliest moments, we've received the message that our appearance is an important—if not *the* most important—thing about us, and if we're not perceived as attractive, then we won't be accepted and loved.

At the root of all body-image struggles is the deeply ingrained belief that our looks matter . . . a lot. To undo this conditioning, you must remind yourself that being attractive is not your purpose, nor is it a prerequisite for a good life. Despite what you've been fed, your appearance is not that interesting or important; it's nothing compared to the depths of your heart and the light in your soul.

Consider who or what made you believe that your looks matter. Now that you're evolving, what do you believe is more important than your appearance?

body

Gain Confidence Through Competence

Confidence isn't gained through chanting positive affirmations. Though those might momentarily hype you up, they create cognitive dissonance in the mind—a gap between what you're saying to yourself and what you truly believe.

Lasting confidence is built through competence. For example, instead of trying to affirm your way into body acceptance, start exposing yourself to bodies of all shapes and sizes, diversifying your social media feeds, and learning about the harmful effects of fatphobia. Or if you want to become more confident at your job, focus on building new skills and challenging yourself with growth-inducing projects.

When you build your competence and become better at something, you will inevitably feel more confident. And you don't have to be excellent right away—just knowing that you're en route to becoming better is often enough to boost your self-esteem.

Where in your life do you feel most confident? Where can you work on your confidence, or competence, further?

mind

Romanticize Your Life

Social media is rarely a source of hope, but the "romanticize your life" trend—people filming themselves enjoying mundane moments like pouring coffee, riding the train, and reading a book—inspires me. Romanticizing parts of their lives that are anything but glamorous helps recast their outlooks on life and show that there's beauty in ordinary moments.

When I was going through hard times, I used to take long walks down by the river, often pretending that I was the main character in a movie, admiring the scenery as I listened to melancholic music. Sometimes I cried tears of joy because, despite my sadness, I began to notice the beauty of the world outside my own sorrow. At first, I just pretended to appreciate my life, but eventually I started loving it and, in turn, myself.

You might think that your life is ordinary, but what's ordinary to you now is part of your unique journey to self-love, and that is extraordinary. Write about a day in your life as if you were the main character of your favorite movie.

heart

Strip It Away

~~~~~~~~~~~~~

If you're struggling to find your purpose, it might be helpful to highlight what your purpose is *not* and strip it all away. Your purpose in life is not to be pretty or proper or perfect. It's not to work forty hours a week, fifty weeks per year, until you're sixty years old, left wondering who the hell you gave your precious time to. Your purpose is not to get a job out of college, get married in your twenties, buy a house by thirty—just in time to have a baby—then save for retirement in your forties, and resist aging in your fifties. Those might be worthy goals for you, but they do not amount to your true purpose.

Your purpose is not a place to arrive but a reason to keep going.

So then, based on what your purpose is *not,* what do you think it *is*?

Separate Struggle from Identity

When we tell ourselves stories about ourselves for long enough, they inevitably become part of our identities. For many years, I told myself that I was a binge eater, words that perpetuated my behavior. I kept on binge eating because it was so deeply ingrained in my identity. When I started telling myself instead that "I am struggling with binge eating," I began to detach my struggle from my identity.

Self-talk is so important in the practice of separating your struggles from your identity: you will live by what you tell yourself, and thus, become it. Although there are exceptions in which some may need to embrace their problems as integral to their identities in order to heal (for example, someone who struggles with alcoholism may need to call themselves an alcoholic to confront their problem), there are many identities that we can release if they're not serving us.

What struggles have become a part of your identity? How can you separate them?

Determine Your Non-Negotiables

When I was in a dysfunctional relationship, still figuring out my boundaries and healing from my struggles with self-worth, I often turned to my friends for advice. After another blowout fight with my then boyfriend, my best friend told me that all relationships are hard, but some are *worth* the hard. "But how do you know if it's worth the hard when you're just so conflicted?" I asked. Her take was that when the good times outweigh the bad, it's worth working on the relationship.

This isn't the only litmus test for relationships because everyone has different boundaries. You must decide your own criteria for determining whether a relationship is serving you or if it's sucking you dry. Remember: sometimes love isn't enough. There must also be mutual respect, compatibility, and whatever else is on your list of non-negotiables.

What is non-negotiable to you in relationships? Are the people in your life meeting those criteria?

Ritualize Your Routines

Although research and debate around the meaning of life is seemingly endless, social scientists tend to agree on one thing: routines add meaning to our lives.

Many of us mistakenly believe that it's the big moments, like graduations, promotions, vacations, and weddings, that make life meaningful. But despite their importance, we all know what it feels like to achieve a milestone only to be left thinking, "What's next?" When we're constantly chasing the big things, we miss opportunities to enjoy the ordinary moments that truly make life meaningful.

By establishing routines, you create a sense of coherence in your life, which our bodies and brains seek. It's calming to know what's coming.

What do your daily, weekly, or monthly routines look like? Your routine does not have to be rigid nor strict nor perfect. Instead, think about what you're already doing. How can you add, take away, or find more consistency to ritualize the process?

Trust Your Body

Our bodies have innate wisdom that informs us when we're hungry, tired, angsty, in pain, or off-balance in some way. Unfortunately, many of us have learned not to trust that innate wisdom. Diet and weight loss culture tells us what, when, and how much to eat. Hustle and grind culture tells us not to rest until we're burnt out. Messages that conflict with what we feel at our core often result in feeling even more disconnected from our bodies and constantly searching outside of ourselves for answers that can only be found within.

Learning to trust your body fits into the bigger purpose of learning to trust yourself. The more you practice eating intuitively, resting before you're tired, and approaching health concerns with compassion, the more in tune you'll feel with yourself as a whole. Your body is constantly communicating with you, and it's time to start listening to its innate wisdom.

Do you trust your body to ask you for what it needs—food, rest, relaxation, movement, touch? What is your body asking for today, and how can you honor that request with self-love?

body

Name Your Monkeys

"Monkey mind" is a Buddhist term used to describe the useless chatter in our heads, the sporadic swinging from one branch of thought to the next. Buddha himself painted this visual that never fails to make me laugh: a mind filled with dozens of drunken monkeys jumping around, screeching incessantly, begging for attention.

I like to think of each monkey as representative of a negative emotion, named according to what I'm struggling with. For example, my Insecure Monkey is a self-absorbed drama queen who wants everyone to like her, while my Fear Monkey is a timid accountant who believes that control is the antithesis of failure. This process helps create some distance between ourselves and our harder emotions, while also breathing some humor into them. We can let all the thoughts and feelings pass through us without gripping their tails.

What monkeys are partying in your mind lately?

mind

Zoom Out

~~~~~~~~~~~~

When I get tangled up in thinking about my own identity, I like to imagine the Universe in its entirety. It contains *everything*: all the planets, stars, galaxies, light, and space. I am part of that. You are part of the Universe, as is everyone and everything around you.

While trying to figure out our place in the world (and avoid an existential crisis while we're at it), it's easy to get caught up in the minutiae and forget that we are all part of a greater whole. We get caught up in perfecting tiny parts of ourselves, forgetting that they're just that: tiny parts of us. Instead of poking, prodding, and criticizing every aspect of ourselves, we must recognize that we are whole human beings who experience joy and pain, love and loss, success and failure, pride and despair, and everything in between.

And when that's not enough, zoom out even wider to see that you are a tiny speck of the most extraordinary phenomenon: the Universe. In the words of Eckhart Tolle, "You are the Universe experiencing itself, very briefly, as a human."

List five phenomena or experiences that help you zoom out and see the whole picture.

heart

Push Your Comfort Threshold

You know you shouldn't text your ex, but you do it anyway.

You want to achieve certain goals, but you give up when things get hard.

You're trying to build a positive new habit, but you easily slip back into the old ones.

All these scenarios have one thing in common: your brain is torn between wanting to be challenged and craving to be comfortable, since the primitive part of our brains too often perceives new or unknown situations as threats.

Before I host a retreat or speak on stage—or even release a new book—I always feel like I'm about to throw up. Everything in my body screams, "DANGER! NEW! UNFAMILIAR! SCARY! STOP!" But rationally, I know that there is no physical threat, only the fear in my mind. Once I get comfortable being uncomfortable, feel the fear but go for it anyway, the nerves subside and next time, it's not as scary. Continuing to push our comfort thresholds is the only way we grow.

Where can you push your comfort threshold for the sake of your purpose?

Add Color to Your Beliefs

A lot of the limiting beliefs we hold about ourselves come in hypothetical "if, then" statements.

If I struggle to find a romantic partner, then it means I am unlovable.

If I'm not working productively, then I'm a lazy failure.

If I don't look or act a certain way, then no one will accept me.

Over time, these beliefs become part of your identity. You'll notice that these beliefs are often black and white: one cause leads to one dramatic effect, with very little space for the in-betweens. Thinking in absolutes holds you back from experiencing the richness of yourself, your relationships, and life in general.

The opposite of black and white is not gray. It's every color that you can possibly imagine. No matter how many black and white lies you try to tell yourself, there are even more dynamically hued truths that are much more reflective of reality. Don't reduce yourself down to boring, blanket hypotheticals. You are a complex, colorful, multifaceted rainbow.

What "if, then" statements do you tell yourself? How can you reframe them with more color and nuance?

identity

Embrace Loneliness

~~~~~~~~~~~

Loneliness is an inevitable part of learning to love yourself; it's the space between figuring out who you are and knowing that you are worthy of connection. Loneliness has less to do with the company you keep and more to do with a shift in your life—a shift in thinking, in doing, or in being—when you haven't fully accepted the change yet. You might feel disconnected because you haven't given yourself the time, space, or grace to connect with yourself.

You don't have to resist loneliness, but rather embrace it as a healthy part of self-love. When you're lonely, that's when you have the opportunity to understand and accept the person you're alone with—yourself. Loneliness is not a problem to be fixed but a feeling that, once fully felt, is a gateway to greater connection with yourself.

Describe the feeling of loneliness. When do you feel most lonely? Do you tend to resist it? What could you learn about yourself if you embraced loneliness as a part of self-love?

people

Be Mindful of Self-Fulfilling Prophecies

Imagine waking up on the right side of the bed: coffee the perfect temperature, tank full of gas, your favorite songs playing on the radio as you speed to work with no traffic, and your boss pays for lunch as appreciation for your good work. How would these circumstances influence your mindset? Would they brighten the rest of your day?

Now imagine the reverse: you sleep restlessly, stub your toe getting out of bed, burn your tongue on coffee, get stuck behind red lights as you rush to work, only to be greeted by a cranky boss and demanding coworkers. Would that cast a cloud over the rest of your day?

Both are examples of self-fulfilling prophecies—fun when they work in your favor but not when they perpetuate a chain reaction of doom. Though we can't control all of our circumstances or the actions of others, we can carefully choose our thoughts to interrupt negative self-fulfilling prophecies and create more positive ones.

What are three recurring negative thoughts that spiral into a negative self-fulfilling prophecy? What are three helpful habits or thoughts that steer you into a positive self-fulfilling prophecy?

habits

The Ocean

~~~~~~~~~~

When I'm feeling insecure in my body, I remind myself of this:

Everything on this planet has
different curves and shapes
bumps and lumps
rolls and folds.
Just think of the ocean.
She has curves just like you
and waves that rise
with the wind.
She moves freely
letting nothing control her
if only the sun and the moon.

And that's you, too.
You are like the ocean
no longer apologizing
for your depth
no longer hiding
all your power
no longer afraid
to take up space.
You are no different
than the ocean,
than nature herself.

Spend time in nature today while reminding yourself that you are nature, too. What aspects of nature make you feel grounded, connected, and at peace with your body?

------

body

Select Supportive Thoughts

Supportive self-talk is how we continuously practice self-love. We're used to telling ourselves: "I can't control my thoughts," and that's true, to an extent. We can't control the primary thoughts that pop into our minds because those are automatic and reflect what we've been taught—by our parents, peers, media, culture, and society. It's important to remember that these thoughts are not our own; we've just repeated them to ourselves for so long that they feel like they're ours.

For example, if I'm feeling guilty for taking time off work, I might think, "I'm so lazy. I should be doing something useful." That's because I've been trained by hustle culture to value productivity more than my own well-being. But I can practice better self-talk by consciously choosing my secondary, or follow-up, thought: "I don't have to unceasingly work to prove my worth. Rest is important and worthwhile." The more we select more supportive secondary thoughts, the better at self-talk we'll get. Eventually, the new thoughts become more automatic than the old ones.

What are some unsupportive automatic thoughts that pop into your mind? How can you reframe your self-talk into more supportive, self-loving thoughts?

Choose Love Over Worry

Years ago, I attended a psychic workshop for fun led by a teacher named Angel. During the class, a woman shared that she was worried about her daughter. Angel addressed the class: "How many of you are worried about someone right now?" She prompted the half who raised their hands to sit together in the center of the room with the rest of us forming a circle around them.

"Those of you sitting on the inside, think about something you're struggling with right now . . . Now those of you around them, start worrying about them. They're struggling, so you must worry about them!" After a few minutes, Angel asked, "What did it feel like to have all these people worry about you?" Participants called out, "It made me feel bad," "Icky," and "Unhelpful." Angel repeated the exercise, but this time she guided the outside circle to send *love* to the worriers. The entire energy of the room shifted dramatically—giving and receiving love is much more empowering than worry. Choose to send love.

Is there anyone, maybe even yourself, whom you can send love to right now?

heart

Meander the Meadow

There is a lot of pressure out there to find one's "purpose," which is usually social code for a job that's relatively impressive, pays well, is easy to explain in one sentence, and bonus points if you're "passionate" about it. I want to reassure you that it's okay if you don't know what you want to do with your life. It's okay if your journey is filled with bumpy roads, curvy paths, and frequent stops. Getting off the beaten path and meandering your way through life is so much more interesting than sitting in traffic, just like everyone else, waiting for someone or something to give you permission to move forward.

Your purpose is a balancing act between embracing what you're naturally good at and exploring what both challenges and excites you. You can't do any of this unless you give yourself time, space, and grace to meander the metaphorical meadow and see what ignites a sense of curiosity. Lost in the meadow of opportunities is a beautiful place to be.

As you're meandering, you might ask yourself, what's interesting to me? What comes easy to me? Who or what or where do I keep coming back to? But remember that these questions are only something to keep you entertained as you meander the meadow.

See Everyone as a Projector

People's negative opinions or judgments are simply projections of their own insecurities. But it's usually easier to recognize this in others than to see this behavior in ourselves. We are all mirrors of each other. Everything we think, say, and do is a projection of how we feel inside. So, when you catch yourself judging someone, it's likely because you have not yet healed that part within yourself. And when you see a trait you admire in someone else, it's likely because you recognize that potential in yourself, too. Once you acknowledge that everything is a mirror, you reclaim your power and stop blaming others for how you feel. Instead, you gain the tools to address the parts of you craving your awareness, compassion, and understanding. When you get into the habit of asking yourself, "What is this trying to show me, teach me, or reflect back to me?" you will find inner peace.

Consider aspects of or people in your life that bring up feelings of frustration or inspiration. What can you see mirrored back at you in your feelings about them?

identity

Prioritize Yourself Over the Opinions of Others

During my late teens, I competed in bikini fitness competitions that required constant dieting and exercising for the "perfect body." This lifestyle spiraled into an obsession with food, fitness, and my weight, until I was forced to confront my eating disorders.

One day, desperate for answers, I confided in my naturopath who doubled as a confidant: "I just don't understand why I keep binge eating," I said, cradling a pillow across my lap to hide my stomach.

Her response hit me like a ton of bricks: "Worrying what people think of you all the time is fucking stressful."

I was starving and exhausting myself for other people's approval of my body. My body had served as a scapegoat for all the ways I'd valued other people's opinions over my own well-being.

When you're stressed or feeling out of sorts, the pressure may stem from trying to please others and live up to their expectations at the expense of yourself. What would happen if you cared more about your well-being than other people's opinions?

Choose Your Struggle

Finding your purpose in life is not about choosing an easy, problem-free path that will make you happy all of the time. It's about deciding what cause is worth its inevitable struggle. Would you rather struggle to make, save, and invest money or struggle with debt, deficit, and debilitating financial stress? Would you rather work on your partnership or heal from a heartbreak? Would you rather struggle to pursue your dream or struggle with bitterness and resentment that builds when you're not actualizing your potential? There is no right or wrong answer to these questions, just like there is no right or wrong path to pursue. And sometimes, there are familial or societal circumstances that we don't have full control over, but we must do our best to choose a struggle that forwards the future we desire.

A note on privilege: there are inequalities and systems in society that prioritize the well-being of some people while making it objectively harder for others. If you face such disparities and the never-ending stress that comes with them, please have extra compassion for yourself as you recognize the forces that are outside of your control, while focusing on those within your power.

What struggle are you currently choosing? Is there a different struggle you'd rather choose?

Try the "Loving Kindness Meditation"

~~~~~~

Love and self-love are parts of the same concept. Your love for yourself and your love for others aren't stored in separate buckets, but rather they come from the same well. When you love yourself, you deepen your capacity to love others. And when you extend love to someone else, you project the love that's already within you.

A Buddhist practice called the "Loving Kindness Meditation" harnesses this concept by silently sending goodwill to another person, whether it's a stranger you pass by on the street or someone you love. When you send well-wishes to someone else, it instantly makes you feel good, too. Why? Because when you think about sending love to someone, you're also bathing in that same love yourself.

This two-minute compassion practice is shown to decrease stress, invite connectedness, and foster acceptance of both yourself and others. Try it now. Write about someone you want to send goodwill to. Describe the well-wishes you have for them and notice how you feel.

Release the Resistance

~~~~~~~~~~~~~~~~

Your drunken monkeys (see pg. 134 for a full explanation) don't like to be told "no." If you try to fight your monkey mind and push away negative thoughts, feelings, and emotions, they'll only come back stronger, yelling louder until you give them attention. In the words of Carl Jung, "What you resist persists." The more you try to *not* think about something, the more you will inevitably think about it. The more you feed or fight or try to flee your monkeys, the more they'll come back with a vengeance.

Instead, observe your thoughts, acknowledge your feelings, and process your emotions with self-compassion. Meditation is one way to practice taming these monkeys. The goal must not be to fight them off completely but to make peace with them. To me, journaling is meditation in written form. Whether we sit in stillness with our drunken monkeys or write about them, we gently release the resistance. This does not mean that you act on—or even embrace—your bad thoughts; you allow them to exist, thank them for trying to protect you, and let them float away, passing by like clouds in the sky.

What thoughts, feelings, or emotions are you resisting? What would happen if you gave them permission to be?

mind

Focus on Your Heart

~~~~~~~~~

Of course, we want to accept our bodies and feel at peace in our own minds. But we'll encounter days when acceptance feels harder to grasp, when we find ourselves slipping back into self-criticism, stress, and shame. On those days, repeating this mantra will help to reach outside of ourselves:

I am not my body. I am not my mind. I am my heart.

What's important is not what you look like, how you feel about your appearance, or what's going on in your physical shell because you are not your body. Your body will die one day. And it doesn't matter what thoughts you can't stop thinking or the feelings that are overwhelming you because you are not your mind. Your mind will forget itself one day, too.

When you focus your energy and attention on your heart, you liberate yourself from materialistic illusions and tap into the dimension beyond the "you" that you're so attached to. Your body will die, and your mind will forget, but your heart and soul will keep on living through it all. Your heart is where unconditional self-love lies.

What does "unconditional love" mean to you?

----

heart

Change Your Shoes

One night, in the middle of winter in Calgary as I headed home after my shift at a cocktail lounge, I struggled to maneuver around the snow and ice on the sidewalks. Regrettably, I'd forgotten to bring a change of shoes, so my high heels slipped from under me. I fell flat on my ass, onto an icy road, in the middle of an intersection. My tailbone was bruised for weeks, but the emotional impact of the fall lasted longer.

That night, the weight of my circumstances came crashing down on me: I felt stuck in an on-and-off abusive relationship, struggling with binge eating and my body image, living by myself in a foreign country as a broke student. I sat there, in the middle of the street, crying and feeling sorry for myself until I came to terms with the fact that I needed help. I'd found myself knocked off my feet because my foundation was unstable, unreliable, and unsupportive. I had only two options: keep slipping on ice or change my shoes.

How solid is your foundation? Is the path you're on conducive to your ultimate well-being? If not, how can you change your shoes or walk on a different path?

purpose

Let Comparison Teach You

In her book *Atlas of the Heart*, Brené Brown explains that we usually don't compare ourselves to people who are far removed from our own lives. She shares the example of how, as a swimmer, she doesn't care to compete against Olympic gold medal champions, but she will peep at the stranger in the lane next to her and evaluate herself against them.

Brown calls this the "crushing paradox of 'fit in and stand out!'" We want to be like everyone else but a bit better. I believe this stems from feeling unsure of ourselves and our values. When we don't know who we are, we'll try to figure ourselves out in relation to others, people similar enough to us.

Sometimes, the people we compare ourselves to remind us of what we want. If you admire something about someone and truly want that for yourself, it's time to quit comparing and start creating. But sometimes, you might find you just got caught up in the perceived glamour of others' lives. The antidote to comparison is to let it teach you and reground you in your own values.

Who do you compare yourself to? What is this comparison teaching you about your values?

identity

Look at Breakups as Mirrors

Breakups are mirrors. They force you to prioritize your healing by reflecting exactly why the relationship didn't work. For example, if you left a relationship full of verbal mistreatment, your healing should focus on how you speak to yourself (i.e., self-talk). If the relationship lacked sexual, intellectual, or emotional intimacy, then you have an opportunity to explore the depths of your own sexuality, mind, and emotions. Conflicts about money or lifestyle are catalysts to become financially stable and to live out your dreams, trusting that a future partner will only add to your already full life.

As you look in the mirror, you may grieve the loss of your ex and your imagined future with them, but if you look hard enough, reflected back will be the parts of you that you'd lost in the relationship.

Ask yourself, how is this breakup a mirror to where my healing lies? How can I rebuild the parts of myself that I lost in the relationship?

people

Check the Conditions

While studying in Calgary, I worked evenings at a seedy cocktail lounge in the city—the only job with hours compatible with a full-time student. Checking coats and seating guests late into the night, I tried to fit into nightclub culture. I kept quiet as my boss told awful jokes, often sexist and racist, and I made amicable small talk with the misogynistic bouncers to avoid conflict.

Surrounding myself with those people made me into a person I wasn't proud of. Although I thought my character was strong enough to resist turning into someone I didn't respect, my environment influenced me. But looking back, I try not to blame myself: When a flower doesn't bloom, you don't blame the flower; you check the conditions it's planted in. If you want to grow and heal and love, you must create an environment conducive to that, and the number one determinant of a positive environment is supportive people.

Take inventory of your environment and the people you spend the most time with. Are the conditions conducive to your healing, growth, and self-love? If not, what's keeping you there?

Apologize to Your Body

Sometimes we owe our bodies an apology for mistreating them when all they've ever tried to do was keep us alive. Here's my letter to my own body:

Dear Body,

I'm sorry for all the years I spent putting you on restrictive diets and exhausting you with endless exercise.

I'm sorry that I didn't trust you when you begged me for nourishing food, joyful movement, and plentiful rest.

I'm sorry for all the hurtful words I said to you, and I'm sorry for all the time I spent loathing you when I could've been loving you.

I'm ready to love you the way you've always deserved to be loved.

Please forgive me.

Thank you.

I love you.

Now write your own apology letter to your body.

_____

_____

_____

_____

_____

_____

_____

_____

_____

_____

_____

_____

_____

Tap into Your Dark Side

When my sister, who is an extraordinary artist, got in trouble for not cleaning her room, she would say, "Mama, it's not my fault I'm messy! It's only because I'm so creative!" I found Ilana's wisdom, albeit sassy, quite inspiring because of how she embraced her imperfections and saw the gifts that lay within them.

Some psychologists would call this a version of "shadow work." First popularized by Carl Jung, shadow work is about tapping into your "dark side," parts of yourself deemed unacceptable by society, to deepen your self-awareness. The practice often requires the help of a professional, but you can start by harnessing the concept of duality.

On the left, write down a behavior or trait that you feel insecure about or judge yourself for. Then, to the right, explore how that behavior or trait is also a gateway to your gifts. For example, I worry that I talk too much. But if I didn't have a way with words, then I wouldn't be able to host the Mary's Cup of Tea podcast or write books for you. There can be no shadow without a significant amount of light—that's the beauty of duality.

mind

Find Light in the Darkness

At night, when I step outside from a brightly lit room, it always seems so dark that I can't see anything. What I'm seeing isn't darkness itself, but rather the absence of light. True darkness doesn't exist; even in darkness, there's light all around us that we can't see because our eyes are limited to seeing photons in certain wavelengths. This is a great metaphor for life. When we're in the "dark," feeling sad, lost, or lonely, the problem is not the darkness but our inability to feel the "light"—happiness, joy, connectedness—in our current wavelength.

When I'm lost in the dark, sometimes I seek outside help, the candles and flashlights of this metaphor—therapy, medication, or self-help resources. Other times, when I look up at the sky, I realize that the brightest stars are only visible in the darkest skies. Surrendering to the experience can be freeing, and eventually I find beauty in the light I can see.

Remember that just because you can't perceive the light right now doesn't mean it's not there. What measures have you taken to find the light in your own dark times?

heart

Let It Be Easy

~~~~~~~~~~

My brain likes to overcomplicate everything I do. Sometimes even the smallest task, like texting back a friend, feels daunting, let alone tackling big projects, like hosting an international retreat or planning my wedding. When you feel overwhelmed, tell yourself the following:

Yes, you are overthinking it.

No, you do not need to have everything figured out to take the first or next step.

Yes, you're making it more complicated than it needs to be.

No, not everything has to "make sense" to everyone.

Yes, you are capable.

No, you cannot control every possible outcome, no matter how hard you try.

Yes, it can be easy if you let it be.

If this were easy, what would it look like? Answer that question and see what possibilities effortlessly unfold.

purpose

Reject "Too"

My emotions are too much. I'm too sensitive. I'm too quiet. Too loud. My body is too big. Too small. Too round. Too flat. Too tall. Too short.

Too. We overuse this word, especially when speaking self-deprecatingly. It's a word that invalidates our feelings and signifies a struggle with self-worth. In this context, "too" leads to binary thinking and comparing yourself to an arbitrary ideal. When you catch yourself using "too" in your self-talk, ask, "Compared to whom?"

For example, your emotions are "too much," but compared to whom? A robot? A person with a different experience, perspective, and way of processing? Who told you or modeled to you what the threshold is? And why do you think that they're right and you're wrong?

If someone else says that you're too much for them, maybe they're also not enough for you.

Maybe you're not "too" anything besides too hard on yourself. You are just right. Exactly where you need to be.

Have you ever told yourself that you're "too" something? Compared to whom? Where did you learn this arbitrary standard you hold yourself to?

identity

Don't Be an Askhole

During a therapy session, I was complaining about a petty argument I'd had with my partner, when my therapist interrupted. "Mary, are you being an askhole?" Responding to my blank expression, she clarified: "Someone who asks for advice but then doesn't take it."

My boyfriend had given me what I'd asked for (advice), but it wasn't what I'd wanted to hear.

In that moment, I learned the importance of not only clearly communicating my needs, but also learning to accept when the other person fulfills my request—even if it's in their own way. When people in your life genuinely try to give you what you asked for, don't let your expectations get in the way of accepting their efforts. Sometimes releasing expectations in virtue of inviting in a little more acceptance bridges the gap.

What unrealistic expectations do you have of others? How can you let go of them?

people

Stop Self-Sabotaging

Most people are more afraid of success than they are of failure. It might sound counterintuitive, but our brains would rather experience familiar negative situations and thought patterns than unfamiliar positive situations and self-talk. This is why people self-sabotage; it temporarily feels good to go back to a toxic ex, to procrastinate your goals, and to make up excuses to stay in the status quo. Brianna Wiest, author of *The Mountain Is You*, writes, "Even though we think we're after happiness, we're actually trying to find whatever we're most used to."

It's easy to believe that financial freedom is impossible, that there are no good people to date, or that you're just not cut out for this or that. These beliefs let you place limitations on yourself and stay in a small, comfortable bubble. It's much more difficult to open your heart to new opportunities and expand your perspective. Because once you do that, the glass ceiling will become your floor and you'll be thrown into the unfamiliar yet thrilling territory of success and love.

Where in your life are you stuck in the familiar by self-sabotaging, breaking promises to yourself, or repeating bad habits? What would happen if you gave up short-term comfort for long-term fulfillment?

habits

Live Seasonally

Seasonal living is about connecting with nature and honoring the different phases—whether daily, monthly, yearly, or over a lifetime—that we move through. Slowing down and moving with natural cycles empower us to live life with intention and mindfulness.

It can be as simple as buying more seasonal fruits and vegetables, or as momentous as taking extended time off work during the colder months to hibernate. Here are some other options for embracing seasonal living:

* Work with your menstrual cycle to determine your energy levels.

* Wake up with the sunrise and wind down with the sunset.

* Celebrate dates, such as the autumn equinox, winter solstice, spring equinox, and summer solstice.

* Pay attention to the plants and birds around you and how they change throughout the day, month, and year.

* Feel your emotions freely, as those are often seasonal, too.

* Research the different moon phases and how they affect you.

What does your body need during the season of life you're in now?

body

This, Too, Shall Pass

When we are sad,
we look back on the past
putting ourselves through the pain
all over again.

When we are happy,
we look toward the future
fearing that the joy won't last
that much longer.

Either way, we are
constantly time traveling
in our minds
to a past or future that
does not exist
beyond our thoughts.

The sadness will fade
and the happiness will pass
and the only moment that's real
is the one we're in now.

Knowing that this, too, shall pass
the good times and the bad
the hurt and the joy
and everything in between
none of it will last
which may feel frightening
until you allow it to be liberating.

Describe your present moment. What are you grateful for?

mind

Learn from Everything

Self-love empowers us to see the occurrences in our lives as happening *for* us, not *to* us. This perspective embraces the idea that we can learn from anything. Ask yourself, "What is this trying to teach me?" That is how we shift from feeling powerless in our circumstances to empowered as the creators of our realities.

Every breakdown is the precedent to a breakthrough. Every failure is one step closer to success. Every loss is an expansion for new insights, deeper feelings, and a softer, stronger heart.

This doesn't mean that fucked up things won't happen to us or those we love. Nor does it mean we write off the injustices of this world or avoid the anger that comes from them. We feel the rage, grief, and anguish before deciding that we love ourselves too damn much to keep giving away our power.

Sadness is a nudge *for* you to practice self-compassion. Anxiety is a push *for* you to cultivate inner peace. Loneliness is *for* you to remember that you are all you need.

It's all happening *for* you.

What is happening for you right now?

heart

Keep an Open Mind

~~~~~~~~~~

"The meaning of life is to find your gift. The purpose of life is to give it away." This quote, emblazoned on a giant canvas that was my partner's before we met, now hangs in my home office. For three years, I stared at it, pondering what it meant. It wasn't until very recently that it hit me: self-love! I first had to find self-love within myself to now be able to share it with others. The serendipity gave me chills.

There will be times in your life when everything comes full circle, when things just seem to "click" and all the events leading up to it just make sense. Life is a culmination of seemingly mundane moments and milestones achieved, until you realize that they were all bringing you closer to your purpose. And often, you don't have to try so hard. Let go of the expectation to have everything figured out right away. Follow the clues, stay curious, and trust that everything is unfolding exactly the way it's meant to.

What's a full-circle moment you've experienced recently?

Give Yourself Space to Grow

When it comes to personal identity, there's a nuanced balance between knowing who you are and giving yourself space to grow. Attaching too much weight to certain labels, beliefs, and preconceived notions can preclude future growth. In other words, exploring your identity can help you find clarity about what defines you, but you don't want to confine yourself to those definitions.

Be clear on who you are but allow yourself the freedom to evolve. It's okay to not have everything figured out. In fact, this space is necessary for growth.

What parts of your identity do you find yourself attached to? What would happen if you let that go just enough to leave space for growth? How do you see yourself evolving over the next year, five years, and ten years?

identity

Know When Love Isn't Enough

My first long-term romantic relationship was quite tumultuous, if not borderline abusive. I've talked about this before, but during one of our blowout fights, my ex screamed at me, "I love you, but I don't *like* you." This caught me off guard, but it served as a valuable wake-up call because I realized I felt the same way. I was anxiously gripping onto my love for him, without thinking about whether I even *liked* him.

In a romantic partnership, it's not enough to love someone. You must also enjoy their company and respect who they are as a person. And you need to love yourself enough to know when a relationship isn't good for you, even if there's love there.

Today, ask yourself if there is someone in your life you care deeply about, but who you know deep down isn't meant to be in your life forever. What keeps you holding on? How might you find the courage to let go?

Elevate Your Perception of Self-Love

Self-hatred is limiting. It prevents us from living in alignment with our hearts and fulfilling our potential. When we constantly criticize ourselves, letting our insecurities hold us back, we rob ourselves—and the world around us—of our presence.

People are afraid that self-love will make them selfish, failing to realize that hating themselves is the true indulgence. Think about it: who do you think about the most when you're splashing around in a puddle of low self-esteem and self-worth? YOURSELF. I'm not saying this to make you feel guilty but to give you a loving kick in the butt and to invite you to elevate your perception of self-love. If self-hate is limiting and egocentric, then self-love is expansive and generous. Everything you do in between self-hating and self-loving pushes you in one direction or the other, either forcing you to contract into shame or empowering you to expand into compassion.

Which beliefs or behaviors feel expansive to you? How can you embody them more in your daily life?

habits

Welcome Harmony

When people talk about "finding balance" in the way they eat, work, or live in general, they seem to imply that there's some sort of perfect equilibrium, and once we find it, we'll stay there. Rather than search for balance, I prefer to embrace harmony— recognizing that life flows in cycles, with different seasons of our lives demanding different levels of time, energy, and attention. Instead of forcing a perfect balance, we can surrender to an imperfect-yet-beautiful harmony which calls for less forceful sacrifice and more peaceful acceptance.

Right now, my body is craving more rest, but in a month or so, I might feel more energized and active. If this season I'm prioritizing my work, then next season I'll intentionally make time for more play. I also remind myself that I don't have to try so hard to keep my body "in check" because I trust that it'll naturally be where it wants to be if I consistently nourish and treat it with care. It's not about keeping everything regulated and controlled. It's about accepting all aspects of our lives as they are, in a natural, beautiful harmony.

Where can you welcome, embrace, or create more harmony in your life?

Choose Wonder Over Fear

When hosting self-love retreats in the middle of a Costa Rican jungle, I reveled in the humbling experience of living among tropical birds, frogs, and insects. But when the nights enveloped me in pitch-black darkness and unfamiliar sounds, I couldn't help but feel afraid.

Fear can be healthy, even necessary; it's our mammalian instinct, there to protect us. But we often feel fear even when there's no real threat. The owner of the retreat center says that the antidote to fear is wonder—that feeling of curiosity imbued with admiration, when our open minds empower us to put the apprehension aside and discover something new.

When afraid, ask yourself, "What is this fear trying to show me? Is there an actual threat or is it only in my mind?" Then turn the fear into wonder to learn something new about yourself or the world around you. Choosing wonder over fear doesn't mean that we ditch our instincts, but we can find the sweet spot between awareness and revelation.

What have you been afraid of lately that you can start to wonder about instead?

mind

Open Your Heart

Any time we open ourselves to someone else, we enter vulnerable territory. We risk rejection or—even worse—being ignored. In attempts to protect our hearts, we reject ourselves and our needs before someone else can reject us. We ignore our feelings before someone else can ignore them. We close ourselves off from love, hoping that our emotional guard will keep us confined in the safety of what we know.

But the more we withdraw and push away love, the more we spiral into self-induced alienation, avoidance, and anxiety. That's what happens when we deprive our human heart of its lifeforce.

On the contrary, when we open our hearts and allow ourselves to both give and receive love, we risk getting hurt. But that hurt is no more painful than becoming disconnected from ourselves and the world around us. The world that's begging to see us, to hear us, and to hold us. The world that wants to love us, if only we let it.

How can you open your heart to practice giving and receiving love?

heart

Know That You Are
Whole and Complete

~~~~~~~~~~

As you sit with today's prompt, know that the self-love journey never ends; it only evolves. I want to leave you with this poem to remind you that self-love is already within you.

i hope you find someone
who showers you with flowers
and gives you a love
that feels like roses

i hope you find someone
who holds you through
the dark times and
celebrates you through the light.

and i hope you find someone
who reassures you that
your beauty goes beyond pretty
that your mere existence is enough

and that, yes, you are easy to love
no matter how difficult you feel

but most importantly,
i hope that someone
you find is yourself,
you are your own lover,
your own best friend,
your own forever.

that someone is you
it's always been you
with you, hand in hand,
whole and complete.

How can you show yourself love today and validate that you are whole and complete?

_____

_____

_____

_____

_____

_____

_____

_____

_____

heart

additional notes to myself

additional notes to myself

additional notes to myself

additional notes to myself

About the Author

Mary Jelkovsky is the author of the bestselling book, *The Gift of Self-Love*, and host of the top-rated *Mary's Cup of Tea Podcast: the Self-Love Podcast for Women*. Over the past five years, she's been leading worldwide self-love retreats and her message has been highlighted in TEDx, *Teen Vogue*, *Shape*, and *Health* Magazine. By openly sharing her personal journey to eating disorder recovery and self-acceptance, Mary has inspired millions to accept their bodies and love themselves unconditionally. When Mary's not writing, podcasting, or hosting retreats, she is spending time with her little sister Ilana, who is her biggest inspiration.